AF487851

Tales of a Little White House

Walter W. Bannon

Copyright © 2012 Walter W Bannon

All rights reserved.

ISBN: 9798635339411

DEDICATION

To all of those talented builders that make their work
look so easy. I salute you.

CONTENTS

ACKNOWLEDGMENTS

Thanks to Marilea M. Bannon for editing and proof reading.

Preface

Albeit, the term "White House" may be recognizable as being associated with the home of American presidents dating back to the late eighteenth century, this story is not at all about presidents or politics. This book tells the story of another white house, a much smaller and more humble house with no fame at all. It is a feel-good, heart-warming story with not one iota of content relating to the U.S. Government. You'll read about how a small abandoned and lonely cape, through many twists and turns, unwittingly and surprisingly ended up becoming my sunset-of-life palace. It's a comical journey of events that magically transformed a dingy derelict into a loving lodge.

It was never on the radar screen of my wife's long-term goals to retire into the barren rooms of this forgotten property. I hadn't given very much thought about how or where I would settle down as I got further away from my mid-life years either. One look at this home where it sat suggested it would be a great candidate for a fireman's muster, basically a burn practice. The shingled roof was crumbling, the basement windows were all boarded up, the paint was blistered and chipped, and road soot covered all of the window glass. My first look at the inside immediately brought to mind the oft-heard phrase, "If walls could speak." I wondered, but didn't want to allow my mind to venture too far into what all of these abused walls were saying.

Thousands of vehicles drove past this spectacle every day with few drivers ever paying any attention to the old abode of some long forgotten dweller. I suspect those who did notice it probably wondered why the town hadn't demanded that the owner of the property have it demolished. There are laws about such blight in many communities in Maine.

Nailed across the front of this abandoned house's highway-facing door hung a large hand-painted sign written in huge letters with a paintbrush dipped in obviously left-over pinkish-brown paint.

"Free House-Must Be Moved."

Regardless of this old home's sad state of existence, I saw some potential in it, a pearl of great value, and thus began our strange journey, a trek of which the outcome blows my typically logical mind every single day. Seemingly, with every week that passes, we find ourselves telling our surprising story to a variety of listeners. It may be an electrician, a painter, a family member, a small group of work associates, or simply just curious passers-by wondering when this home was built or what the interior looks like. It's a story we love to tell over and over. Now we throw open our doors and share the ups and downs of our crazy adventure with you.

We hope you enjoy the stories of our challenges and laughable successes as you tour *The Tales of a Little White House*

Introduction

Atop a cunning and unassuming little knoll bordered by the most peaceful imaginable rural Maine setting sits a little white house with a very interesting story to tell. Curiously, the tiny plot of ground that it proudly sits upon hasn't long served as the resting spot for this home. The history of the land goes back many years. Exactly seventeen-seventy-two is the year that historical records show activity first taking place in this locale.

During the early to mid-1700s, Massachusetts was a very large state. Many of the able men living there served in army regiments fighting for protection from the indigenous and for freedom from other European countries' influences. Following the wars, instead of cash being given to these soldiers, land grants were sometimes deeded to them in the more northern, unsettled reaches of their large state. Several courageous men visited this serene area of woodlands that hosted fertile fields and pristine lakes cradled between the Atlantic seacoast and the White Mountain foothills. This snug river valley was originally called "Pondicherry" to recognize the beauty that was spread across the lea between Pleasant Mountain and the ever-peaceful Long Lake. Streams, ponds, and cherry trees were reportedly aplenty (Bridgton Maine 20).

A portion of land was granted to Moody Bridges of Andover, for a township in 1765 as compensation for his grandfather's military service in the expedition of 1690; a failed attempt to capture Quebec from the French. "Bridgestown" became the name of the new grant, later to be shortened to "Bridgetown," then "Bridgeton," and finally "Bridgton" (Bridgton Maine 13).

At the southern end of "Bridgestown" a tiny settlement sprung up on what is now called Willett Brook. The first framed house in Bridgton's southern section was erected here along the banks of this brook by Asael Foster of Danvers, Massachusetts (Bridgton Maine 24). Some historians might argue that the Perley family built the first framed home in South Bridgton before Mr Foster. I'll defer to them to settle this dispute. The

Perley home still stands and has been relocated to Bridgton Center.

This hamlet on the creek grew into quite a successful community with coopers, blacksmiths, farmers, millers, and other proprietors using the small river to power their machinery and to water their crops. Granite slabs can be seen strewn throughout the river bed below this knoll as a testament to the entrepreneurial spirit of those early settlers. At one point in time it is recorded that three dams with mills operated on this little portion of stream flow. These early businesses helped lead to the eventual growth of Bridgton Center as that area of town later developed into a thriving village (Bridgton Maine 30).

One side of the small hilltop where the white house sits is bordered by a brook. The three other boundaries are also easily defined. There is an old cemetery just fifty feet from the back yard border. It is filled to capacity with memories of what life was like before, during, and after the Revolutionary and Civil Wars. It is a stark witness to both happy and sad times. Reading the epitaphs on the smaller slabs of young children, some only months old, gives you a sense of the helplessness many of these pioneers experienced. They often lacked the right medicine to cure even the most common of today's ailments. The sad results are etched in stone engravings throughout this cemetery.

At the fore-yard is a shallow pond created by the slow flowing Willet Stream and a new dam that is within a stones-throw of the knoll's corner. The last dam gave way on April 26, 1996, turning the slow waters below it into rapids and leaving the waters above it only inches deep. At present, the pond is a beautiful pool for egrets, deer, and turtles to thrive in but too shallow and grassy for swimming. I am told that attempts to create a town beach next to the dam back in the nineteen-sixties failed miserably. A local man told me that children refused to swim there because of the many leaches. The murkiness and mud would have been enough to keep me from ever stepping in it.

Every summer, a mother snapper sneaks up to the sandy soil in the knoll and buries her myriad of eggs. Then, when the time is right, the baby turtles start their trek back to the safety of the river. Many of them get run over by cars and others get eaten by birds as they scurry out in the open. Usually at least a half dozen are returned to the stream by the neighborhood watch. As each rescued baby is carried to the vernal pool, it is amazing to see how quickly they swim under water and begin to eat the vegetation.

A short canoe trip up on Willett Pond will bring you to the site of those first homes on the creek built by Asael Foster. The long since vacated hamlet with a half dozen foundations evenly spaced around a centrally dug stone-lined well are easily located. I once descended the well in hopes of finding a relic. I didn't find anything in the bone dry pit and exited it quickly for fear of getting bit by a snake. This particular river-bank site ended up being a family plan in futility however, as noted in Bridgton's history book. It is said that the soil there was too sandy for growing food. This early homestead was called, "Hensborough." It is believed that the name comes from the fact that the ground was so poor there that, "Even a hen couldn't burrow in it" (Bridgton Maine 340).

Finally, across the skinny side street called

Pinhook Road, on the sunrise side of the lot, stands a charming church building which originally was built as a one-room schoolhouse way back in the early 1800s. It sits on granite stones cut from a local quarry as do many of the older homes in this small section of town now named Sandy Creek.

It is here, on this abandoned, postage-stamp sized parcel of land, bordered by history on all sides that a meek and dismal home lighted down with hardly any notice one cold winter morning. One look at the property today might have you thinking that the house had been built at this site when the schoolhouse was constructed. Some visitors have stated things like, "I thought this house was always here."

Amazingly however, through an unpredictable and unlikely chain of events, this pairing of two has-beens, (an abandoned home and a vacant lot) has surprisingly led to the creation of our cute and cozy cottage on a hill, a strong and secure shelter from the storms of life. It is a pleasantly peaceful respite offering all who enter warm comfort, as well as an embrace from an era long since passed.

Chapter 1

Life in the Slow Lane

Coming to Maine from the small fishing village of Noank, Connecticut, and living in the busy city of Lewiston when we first moved north didn't quite fit my vision of "Life in Maine." I was often told of wild bear roaming the woods and fish so plentiful that they filled a stringer with every fishing trip. My friends said that wild berries and apples trees, huge lakes, and sky-touching mountains were everywhere in this part of New England. Maple syrup poured from maple trees and Christmas trees could be found in every back yard according to those youthful braggarts after their hunting and fishing trips here. Growing up in Connecticut afforded kids plenty of opportunities to enjoy the outdoors, but I had never climbed a real mountain nor had I ever seen a lake the size of a city. I loved real maple syrup, but that was a luxury our family of eight couldn't afford. And the thought of not needing to go to Sears for a Christmas tree left me with visions of sugarplums dancing in my head!

Those wild stories of what it would be like to live in Maine led me to accept a job offer in Lewiston in nineteen-eighty-two, but barely three years after landing there, my wife and I decided that we wanted to live in a more rural part of the state. All of those grand stories that I cherished in my youth were the reasons why I wanted to leave the fast lane of an increasingly expensive and crowded Connecticut in the first place. I didn't move north to live in another busy metropolis. Western Maine however, held all of the wonderments that I had heard about as a teen. We discovered this to be true after a day trip to New Hampshire. That drive proved that those tall tales of youthful years were quite true.

In this mountainous part of the state, starting shortly after 1982, the federal government decided that due to the areas geological sub-structure, Western Maine would make a great place to store spent nuclear fuel rods. The hard granite ground that rarely is disturbed by earth quakes would provide a safe sanctuary for the fuel to lose its radioisotopes over thousands of years. However, residents of the small towns in the path of this proposed repository were enraged that other vital considerations had been overlooked. They banded together to fight this possible intrusion into their simple way of life. One issue was the fact that the city of Portland, Maine's largest population center, receives its drinking water from the vast watershed that begins in these remote ponds and streams. Sebago Lake is a precious water source that has many protections around its borders. All of the neighboring towns do their best to ensure this clean body of water is kept pristine. The land-locked salmon fishing at Sebago Lake is a widely-known attraction to the area. Consequently, the environmental laws are strictly enforced.

Never-the-less, the ensuing legal battles between

the state, the federal government, and the local towns continued. It was right in the middle of that period that I began to venture out from the city to this mountainous part of Maine to seek a new job and to locate our dream home. On one of those ventures I decided to visit a Bridgton realtor. After hearing of my interest in getting a bargain, he showed me a listing of a three bedroom cape sitting on over an acre of land near a brook and a public park with a large, forty-acre wood lot in the back. The asking price was very reasonable and well within what I thought I would have to spend to find a suitable home. My first visit to see the Sandy Creek house resulted in my return to the realtor to tell him that there was actually not a home located there at the address he gave me. He chuckled and told me to go back and look a little harder. He insisted that I was wrong and said that the overgrowth of brush and trees may in fact be hiding the house.

Feeling like it was worth the time, I returned and drove up a thin dirt driveway with small saplings growing in the middle of it. It wasn't until I reached the top of the gravel drive that I spotted the secluded cape. It was a charming, cedar-sided home with a wrap-around porch.

There were lots of trees and brush crowded all around it but it looked very cute hidden away like it was. I felt right away that this would be a fine place for our family of four and I especially liked the price. The next day I brought the rest of the family to see it. My wife agreed that it would be a nice place to raise our family so we made an offer for it after which, the realtor responded positively to our bid. I wondered then if I should have offered less, but it was too late. Our bid was accepted and we closed shortly after. Our cape house that we owned in Auburn sold quickly as well.

The dead-end road now offered a peaceful setting to groom children. It was definitely, life in the slow lane. I knew nothing of the history of this short road but I often walked the adjacent, wooded trails where an old two-footer railroad train used to operate starting near the end of the nineteenth century. I spent many days digging up old artifacts like medicine bottles and cast iron tools where the locomotives stopped to let out passengers at Sandy Creek Station. Sadly, the Narrow-Gauge train service ended as cars became the better means of transportation just like steamship travel ended when trains became the preferred mode of getting to and from rural areas of Maine. By the mid twentieth century, all of the rails for the Narrow-Gauge railroad system were removed. Walking along these old rail beds after the rain washed away the top-soil I once located a couple of green-glass pony insulators that were used to support the wires for the telegraph system.

I recall several years after living in our home an event that reinforced my growing interest in the historical village. On one quiet evening as I sat on my porch enjoying the peaceful chorus of frogs and crickets, a friend called me and asked me to step outside and listen. I questioned him as to why but he just repeated, "Go outside and listen. "

"Okay, Okay," I bristled back to him.

I stood on my porch waiting, almost holding my breath so I wouldn't miss what it was I was listening for. Then I heard it. And then ten seconds later I heard it again. I was so excited I ran out the door, jumped into my truck and drove to the entrance of Pinhook Rd. There, standing in a consortium of pipes and tanks all rigged together in a sort of crazy-scientist arrangement was an original Narrow-Gauge train whistle on a home-made trailer rig. A rope traveled from the rig to the truck's door so the driver could pull it while driving.

My friend, who is a big train enthusiast, had constructed an air-pressure system that could build up a massive amount of air and release it in bursts to the huge whistle. It was a blast from the past that hadn't been heard around here in over fifty years. It was music to my ears that reinforced the nostalgic appeal of Sandy Creek and all of its historical treasures. It encouraged me to keep learning all I could of the area's by-gone days.

At the entry to Pinhook Road there was a small overgrown knoll that provided a nice resting stop for a tired "archeologist." Walking on it, I could see old granite foundation stones in their place at the top and center of the knoll that appeared to once support a large old structure. Further research revealed that a Free Will Baptist Church was originally built on this plot at around 1834. Later it was used as a community center, a 4-H club, and finally, around 1935, the building was demolished for lack of care (Bridgton Maine 496).

This abandoned lot sported a huge oak tree at the center of the knoll with a load of smaller saplings near the road edge that I would often trim back just to avoid hitting them with my car in passing. I loved sitting at this tree just watching the cars go by. It was a great spot to prank the neighbors also. One afternoon after stories were spreading in the neighborhood of a raccoon getting his foot stuck in a tree in the woods, I had an idea to spoof the locals. I took a large stuffed raccoon and tied it up about 30 feet into the big tree. Attaching a clear nylon string allowed me to move its feet without being noticed. As the school bus dropped off children, I stood there looking up in amazement. Once a few others gathered, I pulled the fishing-line string which moved the raccoon's feet. That got many surprising laughs and cries. Eventually, I told them it was just a joke but it sure was fun to get so many curious looks.

One day as I was reading the community newspaper I saw an ad from the Town of Bridgton. They were trying to unload a few parcels of land and, to my surprise; this little corner lot at the edge of my dead-end road was listed. The minimum bid had to be at least two-hundred and sixteen dollars. That was what was owed in back taxes on the property. According to the town records, there had been no contact with the land-owners for many years. The town wanted to collect taxes on the lot, so selling it was in their best interest. After some discussion with my wife we agreed that I would place a "small bid" for the land. This where it all turned into a wild and crazy adventure with twists and turns that only a roller-coaster lover would find enjoyable.

Chapter 2

The Uh, Offer?

I couldn't believe that the town was offering to sell my favorite parcel of land for only two-hundred dollars. After securing the nod from my wife that we should bid on it regardless of what we might end up using it for, I reiterated how exciting it would be to own this small piece of land on the cutest corner in town. If nothing more, I could place a few chairs at the foot of the large oak tree and our kids could enjoy this tiny parcel of peacefulness for years to come. I thought long and hard about how much to offer for this property that most likely could only ever serve as a picnic stop due to its size. Finally, after wrestling for days on how to bid on the lot I decided that I would bring two checks to the town for my offer.

In my right pocket I'd hold a check for two-thousand dollars and in my left pocket, a check for two-hundred and sixteen dollars. I had an idea to only hand in the minimum amount in the event that I discovered that I was the only bidder, but if I was one of many bidders, I would hand them the right-pocket check. The deadline for the bids to be into the town office was 1:00 pm. I showed up at 12:30 to make sure that my bid would be in on time.

I was very nervous about how to approach the gentleman at the town office since I had never bid for a piece of land at auction before. I walked up to the counter and tepidly said, "Hello, I am here to make a bid on the tiny lot in Sandy Creek." Suddenly I began to sweat because I couldn't remember with certainty, which pocket held which check.

"Oh, um, what lot are you talking about?" He

asked.

"The one at the corner of Pinhook Road," I replied.

"Hold on, let me look that up," the clerk said as he walked to a table with files on it.

Returning, he smiled, saying, "Oh yes, I see that property. Do you have a bid in the form of a check?"

Still nervous, I paused trying to remember, "Was it left pocket big check or left pocket small check?"

I didn't want to pull out the wrong one and have the gentleman think I was playing some kind of game. He was waiting for me to produce the money. I finally just pulled one envelope out and handed it to him.

"Thank you, sir. We will be opening the bids shortly if you wish to stick around."

Trying to look as though it was no big deal to me I answered, "Oh, sure I guess I could hang out for a while."

I waited in the lobby and when no one was

around to notice, I pulled out the envelope that held the other check. My face must have been a little red because I was feeling pretty hot around my collar. I only hoped that I had given him the bigger check. I discretely opened the envelope which revealed that the smaller check was, in fact, in my hands. "Whew, that would have been foolish to lose the property for under bidding.".

In just a few minutes, I would know if I had won the bid, fair and square!

At one-o-clock, the gentleman who received my check, along with several other town officials and several other bidders, filed into a small private room. I followed them in and took a seat at the table. There were three piles of envelopes in front of us facing downward. Each pile represented a lot being sold. One pile had only one envelope in it. Immediately, I heard the nice man to whom I had handed my check say, "This pile has only one check in it. I suggest we open this one first."

I knew that he was pointing at my bid by the envelope type. I tried my best to look nonchalant as though this was just a simple routine purchase, but I'm sure that my anxiety showed through the tiny sweat beads on my forehead. In what seemed like slow motion, he tore open the envelope and read it aloud to all the attendees.

"We have a bid of two-thousand dollars from Walter Bannon for property #1 and there are no other bids for this lot."

Right away, another town official stated, "I propose to all present that we accept this bid."

After all agreed by raising their hands to signify a "Yes" vote, the clerk proclaimed, "Bid is accepted."

Without a warning, the chairman slammed his gavel down onto the large wooden table with a thud that echoed seemingly forever. I wasn't quite prepared for the dramatic "BANG" of that hammer; nonetheless, I managed to keep my composure. I winced however, knowing I could have purchased the lot for just over two-hundred dollars. I wondered if they would now accept the check in my other pocket if I told them that I had made a mistake and had given them the wrong envelope, but I decided to just smile, remain professionally stoic, and try to look happy. The town manager saw my subtle anguish and said to me, "Don't feel bad for offering too much. In a few years, your land will be worth ten times that amount."

It was little consolation that I had just given away eighteen-hundred dollars more than necessary to the town, but I did get what I came for, so I tried to keep positive about the whole ordeal.

I was handed a quit-claim-deed, then I signed some papers and I was off. I wasn't sure whether I should celebrate or cry but, either way, at least I could tell my wife, "We were successful." I was pretty proud to be in possession of my favorite little corner of the creek. That euphoric emotion helped make my over-bid less painful.

With my deed in hand, I drove to the tiny lot and walked to the top of the knoll where I could look a full 360 degrees at the different sites within view. There was the site of the old Sandy Creek Market in front of where the old train station stood across Willett Brook. The dam was bustling below me, and right where I stood were those huge cut granite stones on all four sides. I paced the distance from corner-stone to corner-stone to imagine what the original building here must have looked like. Thirty-two feet by thirty-six feet was the old foundation footprint. Imagining the entrance to the site, I noticed that there appeared to be steps going towards the pond area. Using a steel probe, I poked the soil all around to reveal more granite slabs. These would need more clearing later on to determine their purpose. I was feeling very energized and excited about being the new owner of the lot that sat forgotten for so many years. A curious feeling of history seeped up into my being from the hallowed ground beneath my feet and began to overwhelm me. The fact that I now owned a significant piece of the buried past, present, and future of Sandy Creek called for for a moment of reflection.

Standing there with time to think about how this all happened, I began to imagine what a small shelter would look like up on top of the knoll.

"Maybe a screened gazebo would be cool?" I mused.

I was pretty sure I couldn't place a house on it but

wondered if a mini-camp with a self-contained septic would pass regulations. I had often seen small camp buildings being given away. I began to dream about the possibilities and it seemed that the more I dreamed, the bigger my musings became. This is where my wife always gets concerned about me. I'll get a thought in my mind and I can't let it go. This dreaming gradually grew to a crescendo of ideas that was starting to unsettle the settled half of my marriage.

Chapter Three

BOLO

When I first moved to Bridgton I recall one sunny day when I decided to take a relaxing, sight-seeing drive along the waterfront of Long Lake. Down one remote road, there in a thick swath of oak trees, I spotted a hand-written sign attached to a very cute, A-framed camp.

"Free House-Must Be Moved."
Amazed at the offering, I explored the lovely

cabin and thought about how cool it would be to be able to just pick this cottage up and move it to another piece of land. It seemed just crazy to me that someone would want to get rid of a place as nice as this. It appeared to be in excellent condition, sporting nice floors, a new roof, and many cutely-framed widows. I learned that lakefront property at this location is very well suited for year-round living. The roads are paved, utility wires are strung all along the shoreline and, basically, everything you need to manage your affairs is right here. This was a secluded area one-hundred years ago when many of these camps were built, but today it is prized lake frontage with all of the latest and greatest technologies available. Now this gorgeous camp was to be torn down or given away to make room for a brand new home.

After seeing that darling A-frame but not having my own piece of land to place it on, I kept the idea of moving a free house to a little plot of land in the back of my mind. I felt that the likeliness of a repeat find was very high, and I imagined that someday I would have a free vacation home of my own. Maine had so much unused land. I was confident that with just a little research I could one day find and join a piece of real estate with the perfect camp. I was now prepared for such an event with my purchase of land from the town.

Once I had all of my legal documents in order I began to put the train into motion, including putting out a "BOLO." In translation, that's Be-On-The-Lookout. I was anxious to put my little dream-camp at the peak of the knoll. I began to spread the word to a few friends and family members to keep their eyes peeled for a freebie.

My next order of business was to research the town's requirements for putting a structure of some type on the knoll. This meant that a visit to the code enforcement officer was paramount. What I discovered there left me speechless.

I was told that since there had been a building at the site, albeit one-hundred years ago, that building had been within the towns set-back guidelines. Sure, it had been removed long ago; however, if my foundation plans remained inside the "footprint" of the original building, there would be few limitations as to what I could do. It was "Grandfathered." Basically, I could treat this lot like any other building lot as long as I met all of the current building codes.

Wow. Now my mind was spinning out of control with ideas. My next step needed to be to hire a civil engineer. He could explain to me exactly how a camp might fit onto this tiny spit of land.

I contacted a local company who specialized in creative designs. I figured It would take some real ingenuity to try to fit a septic tank, a leach field, a house, a shed, and a driveway for at least two cars, on what was deeded to me as approximately .3 acres. The professional gentleman that I located was up for the challenge.

We met at the knoll and the engineer walked all around asking me all sorts of questions, most of which I answered with vague generalities since all I had so far was a quit-claim deed. I had yet to see a survey map of this land. I asked the civil man why he thought that a survey was relevant given that each side of my square postage-stamp lot was easily defined. He just answered with a frown. No words…

After about an hour of taking measurements from the hilltop to the four borders, including a walk to the brook and the pond, the nice man stood atop the knoll looking out like I envisioned those early pioneers did after charting the town rod-by-rod over two-hundred years ago.

"I am sorry, Mr. Bannon," the man said.

My heart dropped faster than I have ever felt it sink as I anticipated the regrettable news.

He continued, "This lot is too small for a three bedroom home to be placed upon it."

Now my heart just got picked up, dusted off and recharged with excitement as I replied, "I don't need a three bedroom septic system. I was actually hoping a one or two bedroom septic system could fit if you could figure that out with all of your fancy gadgetry."

"Oh! Well, a two bedroom system would fit tightly on the lot if you use the front slope and the side edge but you will never be able to expand on that."

I was so excited to get that news that I could have hugged him. I thanked him and paid him a couple-hundred dollars for his work. He would send me a formal design in the mail later on. It was now real. It was going to happen. My vision of placing a free home on my dream lot was coming into view. This was the news I needed to release the caged ambitions of my imagination. A new energy coursed through my veins. Like the dam bursting when Willett Brook flooded, I gushed with unbridled hope.

Now unshackled from constraints, my enthusiasm was sky high. Each day that passed was making my wife a little more nervous however. I assured her that hiring an engineer would be just another small investment. She still wasn't convinced it was worth the growing expenses I was adding to our budget. Nonetheless, she went along with my frenetic fervor, albeit, her ambivalence was politely creeping out through her half-hearted smiles.

I, on the other hand, was like a kid in a candy shop now. I was driving down every camp road I could find after work every day. I drove from Sebago to Harrison, around to Standish, and back to Bridgton at least once a week. I just knew there had to be that perfect home that had fulfilled its purpose of making fun weekends for vacationing families but now needed to make room for a new house. I could see it in my mind, sitting there along the shoreline, an adorable camp with two bedrooms and a loft. I just knew it was out there, but I had no idea where it was or how it would be found.

I began spending more time driving all over the area, leaving work at 3:15 but getting home an hour or two later. I only worked seventeen miles from my house, but the trips home now covered fifty to seventy-five miles. My wife never complained and I rarely described much about where I had been. I wanted to keep her level of concern to a low burn. Regardless of my attempts to downplay my rabid hope, she sensed that a storm was brewing.

Chapter 4

The Prospect

Some of the most unlikely events often come to us through the simplest of ways. That might be a good way to explain how this next event moved my dreams of finding a little camp a bit closer to reality. It wasn't by driving endless hours down dusty camp roads, nor was it by my relentless scanning of newspaper ads and internet postings. It wasn't by searching the "Free for the Taking" section of Uncle Henry's Swap and Sell Guide©, nor was it by scanning the back pages of the local newspaper's "Wanted" columns. No, it wasn't any of the typically expected ways which I had assumed would be how I would discover my dream cabin. Is it possible that the cabin of my quest was right in front of me, as plain as day all this time?

One day as my son and I were clearing branches and trees from our little lot, my brother stopped by and asked if I had seen the old home with the "Free House" sign on it. Feeling a bit skeptical since I had already searched every camp road within twenty miles, I told him I had not but that I wanted to go and see it right away. I still felt that every lead needed to be checked out. There was no time to waste. I wondered if this house could actually be the hand for the glove, the butter for the toast, the answer to my prayers.

It was a cold Sunday afternoon that we drove south down Route 302. It's a road that I travel every day. It would take approximately thirty minutes to get to North Windham, where the house was sitting, waiting for a taker. I had driven past this house many times in my daily travels. I wondered why I had never noticed a sign on it. Perhaps it had been placed on the house within the last day or two? The office I was employed at years earlier was perhaps only a mile from the home. I couldn't wait to inspect this unwanted dwelling my brother was trying to define for me.

As we drove together he kept warning me that it may not be what I was looking for. I sensed some trepidation in his words. He said it appeared to be in "okay" condition. He also said it was very close to the road where a new mini-mall and new businesses were springing up. I tried to glean all I could from his descriptions as we drove anxiously to see my potential new home but he had little more to offer that would satisfy my curiosity. I was "chomping at the bit" for more detail.

As we arrived, I parked my car in a dirt opening only a few feet from the highway. Wow, the house really did sit only about ten feet from the main road. Because it was so close it was mired in road dust. Every window was soot covered. It looked pretty rough from the outside. He was right to not get my hopes up too high before seeing it. My first impressions were pretty poor. The basement windows were boarded up, the roof was shredding tiles and the paint was peeling off everywhere.

To add to my concerns, it had a huge brick chimney going up through the center of the home. We walked up to the foundation and poked our heads underneath which revealed that the massive chimney was crumbling at the base.

"This could be complicated," I murmured.

We wandered around to the back of the house following a worn footpath that suggested others had been exploring the home recently too. Turning the handle to the back door we found that it was unlocked. The muddy footprints leading in seemingly invited us to explore as well. Immediately I noticed multi-colored walls with lots of punched in holes. So many in fact, I had to ask why anyone would treat a home this way. I wondered if the last residents were boxers and liked to practice on sheet rock or was there a deeper significance? Were they angry at the landlord for some reason or were they just practicing their Karate kicks on a soon to be demolished house?

I hit the light switch and the single incandescent bulb hanging by two wires from the kitchen ceiling came on. I was surprised to discover the electricity still active. Green and yellow cabinets on thin pine doors with pitted-chrome handles and hinges immediately drew my attention. I thought it was more than a bit odd looking. Green laminate counter tops with aluminum trim screamed a forties motif that could turn any nice looking meal sitting on it into an artwork similar to a Dali painting.

"Cool," I said, turning to notice my brother's expression of disgust. Then I spied an antique refrigerator and did what anyone else would do. I opened it. That was a mistake. It reeked of old food. I reached in to turn the dial to "On" and to my shock, it started running.

"This could be a saving," I said out loud. My brother again looked a bit disgusted. "I wasn't talking about the left-over rancid food."

Walking onward to the bathroom revealed an old claw-foot tub next to a dingy toilet with barely enough space left to stand and wash your hands in the sink. That room was just about five feet wide by six feet long and displayed even more punched in walls. This was a pretty comical sight. I stood in front of the sink and tried to imagine how to use it without the behind-portion of my body leaning over the toilet. Talk about efficiency!

"How cute," I chortled.

We walked through that first floor that had two bedrooms, a living room, a dining room, a kitchen, that teensy bathroom, and a staircase that led to the upstairs bedrooms. We just had to go up and look around even though the thought of a squirrel or a bat flying out at us kept us moving cautiously. At the top of the staircase were the two bedrooms. It was actually one big attic that was split with makeshift walls of paneling. One side was a typical bedroom size but the other shared the space with that giant brick chimney. That left very little room for a bed and a dresser. As usual in this house, the sheetrock was in poor shape and would all have to be removed if I were to take it. Still there was a curious charm about this small house that was beginning to taunt me. It had a sort of early New England cape style that I thought just might go pretty well with my lonely site.

I pushed my hands into holes in the ceiling and each time I did, I found solid, rough-cut hemlock framing. These were real two-by-fours; unlike the ones they build houses with today that measure meager three and a half by one and a half inches. No matter where I poked, this house didn't have a single bit of soft wood anywhere. When I had checked the floor structure in the basement, it was similar. There was no rot. The oft-exposed roof rafters were rough cut two-by-sixes and were in perfect condition. With all of the framing in excellent condition, and the fact that it had newer vinyl, double-hung windows everywhere, I was beginning to really like it. Forget those ugly holes, they can be patched. Forget the old BX tube electrical wiring used in the the forties. That can be replaced. This was a solid framed, World-War-Two era cape that was built like a tank. The roof rafters were so strong that they were spaced two-feet apart instead of sixteen inches on center. There was no plywood used in the construction of this home. It was all sided and roofed with one inch boards that were most likely milled locally. What we had here was a shell that could become a beautiful cape. A little remodeling could fashion this into a sweet two bedroom home.

I was trying to imagine this little house on my plot of land and, although it was bigger than the camp I had envisioned, I felt that this old homestead had potential. The measurement of the foundation was thirty-two feet by twenty-six feet. That meant that it would fit inside of the old foundation's footprint. It also meant that it would take a professional mover to transport it. That mattered little to me as I had a growing confidence that this was my dream home. I was ready to go and talk to the owner the very first thing on Monday morning to tell him, "I'll take the house.

There was one great concern however that would need to be addressed. The problem was how I would transport this building that stood at about twenty feet tall. The wires that traverse the major highways are often only between eighteen to twenty feet over the center of the roadway. If I had to lift the house another two feet to sit it on a trailer, that would put my peak at twenty-two feet. Having worked for a utility company, I knew that the cost for linemen to lift or lower cables is extremely expensive. Considering this home needed to travel twenty miles meant that the cost to transport it could be tens of thousands of dollars. That wasn't an option. After all, it was supposed to be a "Free Home."

I processed several ideas in my mind as to how we could get this house to my lot without spending a ton of money. Perhaps cutting it in half, then laying each side down on a trailer would work? Maybe picking it up with a helicopter was an option? I could possibly chop the roof off and replace it with a new roof? I didn't know how this issue could be resolved, but I knew someone who could figure it out. It was time to consult with my friend that was well versed in dealing with challenging building situations. He had lots of experience with these types of issues. I was certain that he could do it. I also figured that it would be much cheaper doing it his way.

Chapter 5

Reality Hurts

The first order of business after returning from the house viewing was to share my enthusiasm with my wife. Let's just say that I had to overcome a mild measure of skepticism, but after telling her about how cool the cape was, and that I thought that I could do this project for only about ten-thousand dollars, she agreed that it might be worth getting and even suggested putting a full foundation under the home instead of a slab. It would make the home much more livable. I was very excited about that possibility.

Monday morning found me eager to visit the house's owner whose phone number was posted on a window inside the colorized kitchen. I contacted him and told him that I was on my way over to discuss the house that he had posted the sign on. He agreed to meet me right away.

Upon arriving at the gentleman's office, I faced a soft-spoken man who didn't seem to believe that I was prepared to take his house. I told him that I had looked it over on the weekend and that I would like to own it.

"Yeah, you and a dozen others want that house. Everyone wants the house but no one has a place to put it!" He said.

Angrily, he stated that one group even had the nerve to ask him to hold onto it while they looked for a piece of land to place it on. A good bit of frustration was detected in his response.

I simply replied, "I have a piece of land that is just perfect for the home and I am ready to take it. It will be a perfect match for my little lot."

He seemed a bit more relaxed and wanted to know more about my land. After explaining to him how

I acquired it, leaving out the part about the two checks, he told me that if I were to take ownership, I would need to remove it ASAP. He wanted to prepare the area for another commercial building and the house needed to go quickly. I assured him that I would start the process immediately. We shook hands, he typed up an agreement, and I signed on the bottom line. Getting a free house made me feel better about over paying for the land by eighteen-hundred dollars. This transaction sort of evened out the pain.

I left his office happy as a clam. While the task ahead was not going to be a small job, I just knew that in the end it would be worth all of the challenges. I have to say, however, I wasn't quite prepared for this next one. I was quickly learning that my "Free House" was not going to be that free anymore and this next hit would be a doozie.

I contacted a house mover in Naples who said that he could possibly move the house but that he wanted to go and look at it first. I told him that was a good idea and that I would await his return call. In the interim, I contacted my friend who had the handyman side-business. He was pretty capable of figuring out how to get through the trickiest of situations. He wanted us to go and see the house together so that we could agree on a game plan.

A few days later, he and I went through the same steps that I had taken with my brother. The handyman however, held a heavy mallet and when he approached the base of the large chimney, he started to slam his hammer into it. I guess he wanted to see if it would come down in place by knocking out the bricks at the base one at a time. He then walked into the house and up the stairs where he slammed his mallet at the chimney again taking note of how it crumbled. Then I saw him counting the roof rafters.

"Twelve." He chuckled. "Only twelve roof rafters! We can number them, slice them at the top and bottom, lower them onto this second floor and wrap this house up like a Christmas present."

"But there are shingles and boards on the roof. How can we just cut the rafters and lower them?" I asked.

"Every shingle will come off and be discarded, then each board will have the nails pulled out and will be laid down in order on the floor we are standing on. When that is done, we will take a saw and cut number one through to number twelve and line them up in that order on top of the boards. The roof will then be re-assembled in the reverse order on your land and a brand new metal roof will be installed after all of that work is accomplished."

"Great, that sounds fantastic," I blurted out. "Will it cost much to do that?" I asked nervously.

"It will be much cheaper than paying utility crews to move wires along twenty miles of roadways," he assured me.

"Okay then let's do it! I will help you, and my brother can help too and together..."

Interrupting me, he said, "I have a crew of two or three that can do the work in a day. If you want to help, you can stand on the ground and pick up pieces of shingles for disposal. I don't want you to get hurt in there. We will take the chimney down from the top of the roof line to the floor, and then we will go underneath and break down the supporting bricks until the rest of the chimney collapses into the basement. We will cut all plumbing lines, electrical lines, and any other attachments to the foundation so the mover can simply, pick your package up and go. You can call the power company and have them shut off the electricity right away if you'd really like to be helpful."

"How much do you think it will cost?" I asked again.

"I will just bill you by the hour and that will be cheaper for you."

"Uh, okay, my wife will be very happy to hear that."   I smiled and we parted ways. The drive back home gave me some time to try to figure out how expensive the cost of hiring the crew was actually going to be. Upon arriving home, my wife said that I had received a phone call from the house-mover. I was nervous about returning the call since I hadn't yet digested the house-prepping cost. Regardless, I needed to move ahead with events that were already in motion.

"Well, Mr. Bannon, I looked at your home and you know it won't be cheap to move.
You will need to pay for two state troopers to escort the house down US Route 302 since it is a state road, and that'll cost you around one thousand dollars for each officer. We can pick up the home with our hydraulic lifts, but I will need a crew of three men to assist me, and I'll

have to pay them each a day's wage. Finally, with all of our equipment and mileage costs, I think I can do this move for you for only twelve-thousand dollars if there are no other unforeseen circumstances. And the good news is that we can do it in another few weeks. Are we good sir?" the fine gentleman asked.

"Oh, yeah, sure, that sounds great, so only about twelve thousand dollars, that's all?" came my crumbling reply. Still trying to get my heart to return to some type of normalcy, I blurted out, "Let's do it."

I don't know what was more difficult, trying to organize this project with multiple contractors or trying to organize my plans of financing with my wife. This unplanned cost was going to be a tough pill to swallow for both of us. My experiences in financial matters included three business ventures. All of them were abject failures and after the last one, I assured my wife I was done trying. In order to soften the impact of these rising costs, I decided to take money from what I had saved in my retirement fund so that the impact wouldn't hit us so hard. Unfortunately, at tax filing season, I discovered that it would cost us thousands of dollars more for taking out that money because of the early withdrawal penalties and the extra taxes I was hit with.

Reeling from reality after that phone call, a shudder traveled down my spine, hit my toes, and then came racing back to my brain. I hadn't estimated the total cost of the foundation yet. I needed to have the foundation and septic system put it before I could move the house. This had to happen immediately. I had heard that a foundation would typically only cost about five thousand dollars. Feeling the urgency, I contacted a neighbor who does foundation and related site work. He was able to get me an estimate right away for digging the driveway, hauling off excess sand, setting the septic tank and the leach field, pouring the foundation, and landscaping the yard, including, seeding the lawn for grass. I was stunned, however, when he told me his estimate.

"Only fourteen-thousand dollars Mr. Bannon," he beamed.

I'm not sure why everyone gives me their estimate for work starting with the word "Only" as though I should celebrate and praise them for keeping my cost so low? This was now just another big-dollar expense that I hadn't planned on. Well, it had to be done and it had to start right away so I agreed to pay his estimate. At this point, I didn't know where the money to pay him was going to come from. Regardless, I asked him to start as soon as possible. Fortunately that was fine for him.

It was now time for my wife and I to do a little financial planning. In truth, it was well past time to do some monetary maneuvering. We agreed that it was time to visit the local bank. The flippant way I had been doing things needed to come to an end. We didn't have a large mortgage on the home we lived in so I was feeling that a small consolidating loan would be a good thing. After all, we really only needed to borrow a few tens-of–thousands of dollars.

Chapter 6

Forty Nickels

The train had left the station, so to speak. It was too late to question whether or not we should borrow money for this project. I had already committed to pay contractors over thirty-thousand dollars and I didn't even have a full-time job at the moment. The company I was working for had a layoff and after almost eight years of working as a technician in antenna manufacturing, I found myself under-employed. With the down-turn in that business and wanting to do some meaningful work, I decided to seek employment with a youth development agency. While I had no formal training, I had the heart for it. I was given the opportunity I had hoped for and jumped right into the job. Although it included working nights, I wanted to learn how to become as good as those others I saw who amazed me with their youth management skills. I enrolled in a study course of behavioral health and eventually became a state-certified "behavioral health professional." I was only working part-time, but the income was very helpful at the moment.

At the same time that I was starting this new field of work, the site planning was beginning. The huge oak tree that sat in the middle of the lot had to be taken down first. I loved that tree but there was no way to set the house on the hill without removing that monster oak. A contractor gave me an estimate of two-hundred dollars to drop it in place. That was two-hundred dollars I needed immediately that I had not figured on spending. Ugh!

As I left work the following morning I planned to meet the tree boys. On my way out the door, a nice lad asked if I would swap forty nickels for two, one-dollar bills. I agreed to the swap but found that forty nickels in my pocket wasn't very comfortable so I stopped at the local gas station and asked the young attendant if I could give her my forty nickels. She said that was fine, and I, being only half awake said that she could simply give me one of those two-dollar scratch tickets. I was sure I wasn't seeing right after scratching off the ticket revealed that I was a two-hundred dollar winner. That was exactly what I needed to pay the tree man. I traded the ticket for two-hundred dollars in cash and headed to the land to pay the tree-cutters. I was reminded in that event that I just needed to relax and not worry about the small stuff.

Back at the land, I soon discovered that I wasn't the only one sad to see the tree go. Some of the neighborhood youth were threatening to stage a protest on my lot for daring to cut it down. I tried to reason with them.

"Sometimes a tree becomes a chair or a table to help us, other times it is cut into firewood to give warmth to a cold home," I said.

That didn't soothe their dismay. They pleaded

with me, but left in a distraught state knowing that I was determined to turn the hill into a homestead. They never did carry out their plans to oppose me; nonetheless, to this day I think they remain unhappy about my actions. It sounds a bit ridiculous that I gave credence to their concerns but, after many years of teaching our youth to stand up and voice their opinions to try to change the world for good, I felt that they were doing only what they believed was right.

Without incident, the old oak tree was removed and the property was flagged with little red markers that showed where the location of everything had to be situated. The neighbor noticed our work on the land and asked if I was aware that his well was located less than one-hundred feet from the flagged septic excavation area.

"I didn't know that," I replied.

My brain wanted to explode at the thought of a problem like this coming up now. I was baffled at how we could have missed this with all of our careful engineering. I immediately contacted the design engineer and he came right over. The neighbor's well cover was about twelve inches under the lawn. You might say, "It was well hidden." I had often seen the neighbor's truck parked on that spot and never dreamed that there could be a well under his truck. It didn't matter now. A careful measurement revealed that in fact, the edge of the leach field was only ninety feet from his water supply. With a few simple adjustments to the septic design however, the soils engineer was able to re-plot the placement of the cement chambers an additional ten feet away. When I asked what the fee was to refile and redesign the system, I feared the worst. Thankfully, he stated, "No charge!" That was a first.

With the tree removed and the modified plans in order, the site work began. The huge excavator began to remove dirt to gain access to the center of the knoll where the foundation would be poured. I wondered what treasures might be unearthed after so many years of this lot being used by so many folks of previous generations. I assumed I would find a ton of old bottles and coins.

After the contractor had completed digging the cellar hole, I approached him to walk around the property. While we were standing there talking about how sandy the soil was, before we even began our walk, I looked down at my feet and noticed a large silver coin. I reached down and picked up a silver half-dollar from 1902. I was pleased to finally get my first return on the purchase of the land. I hoped that there would be many more buried in the ground. Perhaps there was a full bag of coins or gold buried by someone here long ago? I planned to return to the dig site after he had finished his work for the day so I could peruse the lot for any other treasures.

While the site work was taking place the handyman crew was beginning to turn the house in Windham into a neatly packaged box, ready for shipping. When I arrived, it was a bitter-cold morning. The workers were all bundled up and were beginning to remove the roof shingles. I immediately began to pile them up into one location. Once they had torn off all of the shingles they began to remove the long one-by-whatever roof boards. Many of those planks stretched over half of the length of the roof. I imagined that when this home was built, every foot of a plank would be used to save money. Some planks were eight inches wide and others were nine or ten inches wide. Some were eight feet long and some were eighteen feet long. Regardless, the entire roof was an interesting patchwork of sturdy, thick, boards. One-by-one, the old nails were pulled out and the boards were removed and laid in perfect order on the floor.

After the roof was completely removed it was time for the demolition of the chimney to begin. One brick at a time was knocked out of its place and tossed to the ground below. I stayed clear as bricks came flying down in succession like rain. At this point I could only watch and wait. It was much too dangerous for anyone to get near the house. Consequently, it gave me a little time to get into my truck and warm up. When the men finally had the brick structure dismantled level with the top floor, another worker began using a sledgehammer in the cellar to break the massive base into pieces. My brother and I were able to clean up the outside of the home while the others pounded away at that formidable stack. After a couple of hours, the entire chimney was splayed out in a pile of mortar and brick. A huge, gaping hole showed from the basement all the way up through the house to the missing roof.

It was now time to cut the rafters. I was given the important task of numbering them. This was a very critical job and I assume also a good way to keep me out of the way while saws were being used. This was an ingenious approach. Both ends of the rafters were cut, and then they were laid in place on the floor. Once all of them were down, there were left two end-walls that stood up completely unattached. It was an odd site. I wondered how those would be lowered. Then, I noticed a worker setting a ladder on the outside of the wall while another was standing inside the wall. The outside worker used a powerful saw to cut a straight line all the way across the bottom of the end wall. Then the end wall was lowered onto the floor, on top of all of the other boards. The other side was also cut and lowered. It was amazing to see this house now. It measured only about twelve feet tall from the sill to the top of the stacked boards.

The final step was to cover everything with a gigantic tarp. Everyone helped to pull the big blue tarp over the house, and then the contractor tied all of the ends and corners up. It looked like a Christmas package. With a little more clean-up and some ropes tied down, this package would be ready for delivery, and what a delivery it would be.

Getting back to the knoll after our day of hard work at the house, I was struck by how nice the layout looked. The contractor had excavated all of those huge granite foundation stones that supported the historic church building and repositioned them into a large garden box. As I approached him, I think he knew by my smile that I was giddy with approval.

"Did you find any more treasures?" I asked him.

"No, the only thing we found was a partial gravestone." he answered.

"Uh-oh, that's not good," I groaned.

I remembered reading an article that said back over one hundred years ago, some of the graves were exceeding the cemetery boundary and that they had to relocate some of the headstones and caskets. I worried that perhaps during that process they might have missed one. He showed me the headstone now leaning on a tree in the cemetery and I read the dates etched into it aloud. I wasn't able to see any names on it because it was actually only half of a headstone. I assumed that it must have broken off from another stone and had been tossed aside. There were no other remnants nor was there any evidence of any caskets found. I felt like we dodged a disaster that day.

The puzzle pieces were falling in to place, including how we were going to finance this project. I felt like I was now operating on auto-pilot, one day at a time. I really couldn't push anything any faster. I learned upon arriving in Maine many years ago that contractors are more relaxed when it comes to time frames. It doesn't always help to try and push folks who are in no hurry. They'll still operate at their own pace. I just needed to relax, see the big picture, and trust that all the pieces would fall into place over time. And fall they did!

Chapter 7

The Flying Hitch

A couple weeks passed and I still had not heard back from the house mover as to when he would be picking up the pretty little package. The foundation was ready, the finances got some "financial planning" and I was patiently biding my time for the next event. I continued working nights, which meant trying to sleep during the daytime. This was not an easy transition for me. It did allow for me to perform miscellaneous tasks during the day but I wasn't getting much sleep between shifts.

Finally, the call came from the mover.

"We will be moving the house tomorrow morning, bright and early." he said.

I was ecstatic. I had to work that evening so I would miss the entire transport event, but by the time I got out of work, typically eight or nine in the morning, I figured that they would have the house sitting pretty on its new foundation.

The next day the movers picked up the house in North Windham and by 6:00 am they were beginning to roll. There was a police escort at the front and at the back of the house. While this normally would be a great time to move a house, I later heard that several school teachers and students were very upset that they had to wait behind a slow moving building that was being transported up US Rt. 302, taking up both lanes of traffic.

Moving a house down a main road poses many unforeseen challenges. Crossing the bridge in Naples was a slow task since the old turn-style bridge that spans Chute River was quite small. I had never considered how wide the bridges were along the route. Then there was the little bridge here at Sandy Creek, just below the knoll. There, the mover had to post a guide on each side of the house as they eased it through the opening ever so slowly. There was no room for errors here. The house made it through by about one inch on each side.

Arriving at the worksite that morning and seeing all of the commotion gave me a feeling of elation. Sandy Creek hadn't seen this much excitement since the days of the train station mail deliveries. Oddly though, the home was on blocks partially into the road and partway onto the lot. It was also up high enough off of the ground that you could easily walk under it. I asked the mover why they weren't setting it onto the foundation and he told me that the overhead wires were obstructing it. I was aghast.

"Are you kidding me?" I said. "Twenty miles of travel and the only overhead obstruction ends up being right at the end of the trip where the house needed to be lifted up high enough to slide sideways onto the foundation walls? That is unbelievable!"

Everything came to a stand-still. The workers stood idle like statues in a museum. The chief-mover suggested that I contact the telephone and cable companies to see if they would send a crew over to lift the wires. They knew that that was not likely to happen anytime soon so the moving crew began packing their tools to leave for the day. They said that they would return once I had resolved this new issue. Before they left I was able to secure a commitment from the phone company to come within a day, while the cable company agreed to send out a crew within two weeks to estimate the job. Unfortunately, that was not an option. I relayed the news to the moving crew and they proceeded to pack up and go home.

I sadly watched them drive away as I tried to wrap my head around how this could have happened. The reason we cut this house in half was to get below every wire along the twenty- mile course. Now, with a mere fifty feet left to go, the corner of the house was being obstructed by the lowest phone line. I gazed at it from every angle and tried to come up with a way to just push the wires up with a long pole or something but it wasn't possible. They needed to be raised at least two feet on the telephone pole to get the house the clearance it needed.   I labored in vain trying to figure out a way to get past this unbelievable situation but there were just no options.

I knew that it would only take about ten minutes

for the utility companies to drill new holes into the pole and relocate their support brackets. This situation ate at me all evening. My wife watched my discomfort with concern. It suddenly hit me that the wires could simply be detached from the pole and temporarily suspended by a rope. It's called a "Flying Hitch" in utility worker jargon. A temporary hook could be hammered into the pole at the two foot higher mark. After that simple process, a rope could be tossed over the hook and pulled down, which would lift the wires up into place. Then the rope could be securely tied until the line crews could arrive to make this a permanent fix. It's actually as easy as pie.

The next morning I called the mover and told him that he was all set to place the house on the foundation. The wires had been lifted onto a temporary hitch and he was clear to proceed. He was amazed at how quickly I was able to get this done. I was too!

The next morning the movers came and, inch by inch, the workers tweaked the house over the waiting cement structure. Then, with the push of a few buttons that raised and lowered each side using hydraulic jacks, the house was perfectly aligned and quietly lighted down to her new resting spot. I felt like the weight of the entire project was just lifted off of my shoulders with the last push of that pressure-release button. There was my dream home at its final resting place. It sat so cute with its blue tarp draped half way down and white siding showing on the lower half. All it needed now was a red bow on top!

As the building movers were finishing up their work, a utility truck arrived and stated that he had an order to adjust some wires. I pointed to the pole that needed the work done and he proceeded to set his bucket-truck up at the wires. He drilled new holes into the pole and re-attached both sets of wires. It took him only about ten minutes. I thanked him as he parted.

Chapter 8

Snowmageddon

Now that the house sat perfectly upon its new perch, the process of putting the roof back up and closing in the open spaces would be the next logical steps, however, I really wasn't in any big hurry to get this started. I was pleased to be able to just plan out my priorities over dinner time with my wife. Since it was cold and wintery, I decided to relax for a while and hope for a bit of warmer weather to arrive. I figured that if I waited long enough, the snow that collected on the house's roof would just blow off or eventually melt. What I hadn't planned on was what snowstorm after snowstorm created.

The endless storms during February and March just kept piling up snow. The tarp-covered roof was a flat surface that held every drop of drizzle too. Seeing it collect, I began to worry about how much weight the little house could hold. We were now getting hammered with storms that measured in feet, not inches. The multiple layers from the first snowstorm after the house landed at Pinhook, to now, were being compressed down and looked like pancakes stacked on a plate. The first layer had thawed and then refrozen. More storms added more layers. Then a warm couple of days turned the top layers into ice. This was followed by another foot of new snow. It was a cycle that seemingly had no end in sight. Even though the house was built with pretty strong floor joists, I began to get nervous about all of that massive weight.

It's not uncommon to have the accumulated weight of snow in Maine cause a collapse of a roof or a shelter. I had built a slanted lean-to onto my shed at our home after we first moved in, when a massive, two-foot snowfall crushed it onto my bikes and lawnmower. The insurance company had so many collapses in the area that after that storm they simply sent out payments to replace the items. There was no way they could even get to see underneath the snow piles to assess the damages that occurred all over Maine.

I knew that it was important to resolve this issue before even one more snowstorm arrived or else everything I had done to this point could be lost. Feeling ready to tackle this job, I walked down the road carrying my fourteen foot ladder and managed to find a place to set it so that I could climb to the top of the snow pile. This was a challenge in itself. I worried that even the added weight of standing on top of the house could be the proverbial, "Straw that broke the camel's back." Consequently, standing on my ladder, I took one small shovel-full at a time, until I carved out a place to stand and work from. I broke through the ice sheet and tossed the meshed layers onto the ground below. It was a tough job that took several hours of serious back-breaking labor for me to accomplish. I wondered at times if my heart was healthy enough to tackle a workload like this.

Eventually, the entire roof was cleared. I could now rest assured that the little house would survive the remainder of the winter.

Feeling that I didn't want a repeat of this spectacle, I contacted the handyman who had packaged up the home for me and asked if he could schedule the re-installation of the roof soon. With slightly less frigid weather approaching, I felt that he could begin shortly.

Within a couple of weeks, his crew was back in action reassembling the big lumber pile on the top. First, the two triangular-shaped end-walls were lifted and nailed into place. Then each rafter that was numbered in order was lifted and nailed top and bottom. Braces were installed to ensure nothing was going to move. Then all of the roof boards were re-attached and covered with a goopy tape membrane that keeps water from seeping in. Finally, a metal roof was added. It gave the home its first appearance of what the house would look like when completed. I thought it was a beautiful sight even with chipping paint and all its other needs.

The next thing that had to happen was to close in

the basement entry. I didn't want it to become a shelter for porcupines or other un-invited guests. I worked alongside another associate to get this done by installing a door in the entryway. This helped to make the new house at Pinhook Rd. look a lot better. It was very exciting to see all of the repairs and improvements getting worked on now. With a renewed energy, and warmer weather creeping in, we began to speed up our work.

I applied for the electrical service to be activated, after which, a local electrician installed a switch-panel in the basement that allowed for the power tools to be used inside the house. He was able to utilize the many holes in the walls to remove the old BX wiring and install new wires throughout the various openings. One of my favorite moments after the wiring was made to the main floor and the outside light fixtures were hung, was turning on the porch light that faced the historic borough. I left it on all night every night for the first week just to announce that, after almost one-hundred years, there was life again at the top of the knoll. It was my candlelight memorial dedicated to the memory of those past, but not forgotten, souls who once thrived here. I left the porch light on to honor the men and women who made this community a place of comfort for the many folks who reside here today.

Chapter 9

The Sucker-Punch

My daily routine now involved working nights, coming home at eight in the morning, trying to put in some sleep, then putting in some time working on the house before going back to work another all-nighter.

I often went jogging to get in some exercise and even entered some of the local races for a little extra excitement on the weekends. I had recently run a two mile race in Sebago and to my pleasant surprise, came in first in my age division. I was pretty pleased that at fifty-two years old, I was feeling like I was the epitome of health. I could still compete. I hung that first-place medal in a place where I could look at it often and think about how much better I could do with a little more practice.

A few weeks following that race I decided to jog a 5k run around Highland Lake in the town's center. I paced myself as I always do, but after the first 500 feet, I had to stop. I felt nauseated and told the others to go ahead. After a minute of rest I started again but could only jog for a couple-hundred feet before feeling as nauseated as I had earlier. I knew that something wasn't right about this and decided to hold off running until I spoke to a doctor. I scheduled an appointment in two weeks to discuss my concerns with our family physician. This was the earliest I could get in. In the meantime, I tried not to exert too much energy. Every time I did, I felt sick.

The morning arrived when I was to see my doctor, but I had been scheduled to work a day shift. I was able to clear an hour of time off to get this appointment done in the mid-morning. I assured them that I would return shortly to resume my work shift.

At the doctor's office I explained what I was feeling in my chest during exercise. They hooked up a plethora of wires to my arms, legs, and chest to perform their exam. I passed all of the tests with flying colors and was happy to hear that I appeared to be fine, but I still insisted that we needed to look a little further because, when I pushed harder in exercise, I felt nauseated. I wanted to show them how that feeling was triggered so they agreed to let me jog for about two minutes, then, another EKG would be taken. What came next was the beginning of a life changing event for which I wasn't at all prepared for.

The doctor said that he saw something in the test that was concerning him and that he had called the hospital in Lewiston to speak with a cardiologist. He said that the doctors there insisted that I needed to be placed into an ambulance and transported to the Heart and Vascular section of Central Maine Medical Center immediately. I argued that it wasn't necessary to go immediately and that I could drive myself later, but they said that they don't let patients go in my condition. I quickly made a call to work and told them that I wasn't coming back today. I told them that I was being transported to the hospital in Lewiston and asked if they could relay the message to my wife at work.

It was a Friday afternoon when I arrived at the heart center. I had just experienced a harrowing, speedy, ride on a stretcher, down a slew of back roads, in the back of the ambulance. The urgency in the drive was suggesting to me that I was in a much more serious condition than I was aware. I began to have flashbacks of seeing my father lying on a hospital bed after his heart complications. I felt like I was following in his footsteps precisely. He started out at almost fifty years of age with chest pain. He had a quadruple bypass operation before he was sixty years old. He spent the next ten years of his life taking medications, often popping nitro pills into his mouth like candy. At only seventy years old, he passed away from a heart attack. I wondered if this was my fate. I was a broken man. There are no words to describe the fear and loneliness of lying by yourself on a hospital bed waiting to hear what your prognosis is. Questions flooded through my mind at a mile a minute but there were no answers.

Was I going to die? How would my wife and children be after my departure? What about the house that sat there as lonely as I was right now? I found no comfort in my attempts to resolve undone things. I wept at the inability to control events in my life. Everything else in my life had to take a back seat to this new crisis now. It was fall and as I laid there in the hospital bed, I remember seeing the leaves falling from the trees outside hoping I'd get the chance to smell the autumn air once more. I vowed to never take for granted the simple beauty of a falling leaf. I feared never getting that opportunity again.

That evening, I was told that I needed to have open-heart surgery. Doctors advised me that there were blockages in some of my arteries that were sufficient to cause me to drop dead at any time. They called them "Widow Makers." They explained that ninety-five percent of these operations are successful. I had terrible fortune with any type of gambling in my life. It made me ponder what my odds were of a successful operation. I guess I should have recalled that scratch ticket. My chances of survival were certainly better than the odds of winning two-hundred dollars.

They would operate on Monday and they said that I should be out of there a week after that. The news again was devastating. I don't know how much lower I could have sunk emotionally. And foremost on my mind was, who would finish my home project?

Chapter 10

The Long Road Back

I was finally sent home ten days after being admitted to the hospital. The doctors said that since I was so "healthy," my recovery should be a speedy one. In the first few weeks I had a lot of pain following the quadruple bypass operation. Inhaling deeply was still painful. I could barely help myself with daily tasks and was limited to lifting things lighter than a gallon of milk. I struggled with anxiety, worrying that I was having complications from the surgery every time I experienced new chest pains. I wasn't allowed to even lift a hammer to pound in a nail. Ugh! According to the surgeon, it might tear open the stitches in my chest. My wife watched me closely over that rule knowing how much I wanted to get to work on the unfinished home. That depressed me as much as my recurring aches.

The little house now sat unattended. Day after day I waited for the energy and strength to walk down and work on it.

Finally, after eight weeks, I had gained enough strength to do some minor physical work. Over the next few months I added insulation to the upstairs bedroom and loft and did as many repairs as I felt capable of. The little white house was slowly getting put back together.

The return to my part-time job was at a slow pace. At first I worked only one shift to see if I was ready, then I worked two shifts in the week and eventually, three days or nights. I wasn't actually physically ready, but I wanted to get back into action so badly. There were times that I wondered why I was working while I was going through frightening heat flashes and chest pains, yet I powered on. My heart was still trying to regulate to a new normal. In truth, this made every day for me a physical and emotional roller-coaster.

With each week that passed, I was able to do a little more with the house. The walls were fixed, and then some of the floors were replaced. I painted the outside, even standing tip-toed at the top of a twenty-eight foot ladder, propped up in the bed of my truck, to reach the highest peak. OSHA might not have approved of that effort. My sister-in-law in Connecticut gave us a lovely oak kitchen cabinet ensemble which we installed to replace the multicolored ones. With all of this work I was doing I was beginning to feel like I could almost call myself a carpenter, until the day I tried to hold a pencil behind my ear and partially underneath my baseball cap just like those experienced carpenters always do. However, when I leaned over to look at a mark I had just made on a piece of wood, the pencil fell into my coffee cup next to my knee, reminding me that I wasn't quite there yet.

Progress on the house was ongoing but it was still

at a snail's pace. The remodeling, though moving ahead, was also ringing up bills that were more money than I was bringing in from my part-time job. That burden was beginning to wear us both down. The road to recovery for heart patients is a long road and I was essentially at step one of a million step march to regaining my strength. I began to suffer from mild bouts of depression due to recurring effects of my operation and the picture of grandeur I once held about the dream home was gradually dimming. I just couldn't pull all of the pieces together in my still weakened condition.

Seeing the drag that this whole house project was putting on our finances and our lives caused me to reconsider my ambitions. I was faced with an enemy I hadn't ever seen before. It was a left-right combination, a physical and financial beat down, with an uppercut of emotional pain thrown in for good measure. I have to admit, I was staggered. This cascade of trouble caused me to do some serious soul searching. I was far from recovered and our bills were piling up fast. It was then that I decided that the hand which I had been dealt dictated what I needed to do next. I would have to sell the house on which I had devoted so much of my time. My precious home needed to go. The dream was over. The funds that we would gain from the sale of our unfinished home would help relieve all of the added stress we were feeling. I just didn't have the strength to continue the work. It pained me to see my dream fail but I had to think of our future now. After struggling for days with the reality I faced, I did the unthinkable task with a terrible weight of disappointment in my heart. The place I once crowed about from the hilltop was now my dying nightmare. I found it hard to talk about my failed project now. With absolute disdain for all I believed in, I fought against my pride and did the unthinkable deed. I put our precious Pinhook property up for sale.

It took less than two weeks to find a buyer. A nice young couple from Massachusetts wanted a vacation home in Maine and they were willing to pay us close to what we were asking even with the house unfinished. There wasn't even any sheetrock on the second floor yet. Regardless, it was exactly what they wanted. Within a day, we accepted their offer and the realtor began to process all of the required paperwork.

A few days after the sale agreements were signed, I received a call from the realtor asking me if I held a title to the land.

"Sure I do, remember? I purchased the lot from the town and I received the quit-claim deed and the sale documents," I replied.

She informed me that those documents did not constitute a clear title and without that, I couldn't sell the land. She said that she was going to postpone the sale to give me the time to hire a lawyer. She added that the legal aspect of this can be resolved but it takes patience, and in my case, going back over one hundred years to find out who was the last legal owner of this lot. Some early records discussed the requisite that if this land was no longer used by the Free Will Baptists, then it should revert to the previous owners or their heirs. That would take us back to the nineteenth century.

Considering the fact that the taxes had not been paid on this lot in over forty years and that there had been no contact with anyone from the church in over one-hundred years, clearing the title was not going to be a simple quick task. On her advice I hired a local lawyer who told me how the process of getting the title cleared works. I had to laugh when he told me that in fact I would be filing a claim against the last known rights/owner of the land, including his descendants. Yes, I was going to file a claim against Mr. Osborne Chaplain (1810-1860). He was named as the defendant and I was the plaintiff in legal terms. This claim would also need to be published in the local papers. Oh, and just to keep our streak of great price-quotes on track, the lawyer informed us that this was only going to cost us about one-thousand dollars.

Once again, there were no options. In order to sell the house I needed that clear title. In the meantime, the buyers decided that they couldn't wait and they cancelled their offer. Consequently, I went back to working on the house; painting the walls, repairing holes and adding sheetrock to the upstairs. After another month of light work on the interior, I was approached by a friend about letting her rent the home. It was starting to look kind of cute even though there was still a lot of finish work to do. It didn't matter. She was determined to live in the adorable cape on the knoll, and since we needed the income to pay our growing stack of bills, we agreed to sign a one year lease with her.

During her stay we discovered all of the aspects of the house that needed attention. Foremost was the fact that the single gas heater I had installed in the basement area wasn't nearly sufficient to warm the entire house. After the first few very cold nights, the house suffered a couple of frozen pipes because the sill wasn't sealed tightly. The tenant was doing her best to block the drafts from all of the windows and doors but, while it helped, it wasn't sufficient. She strongly encouraged me to call a company that could make the house warmer and even gave me the name of an insulation contractor. Agreeing the home wasn't tight, I made arrangements with a company that sealed the sills and filled the spaces inside the exterior walls with insulation. This cost was just over two-thousand dollars. For another two-thousand dollars, I had an upstairs Rinnai gas heater installed. With the reduced drafts and the new heater, the tenant was much warmer and a whole lot happier.

While I was happy to have a renter that always

paid the monthly bills on time, in a way I was jealous that I wasn't the one getting to enjoy sitting on the porch, listening to the crashing water spill over the dam, or hearing the night-time chorus of frogs peeping in the bog. I tried to imagine what it would be like if I were to live here. I could picture myself walking from the house to the stream below to catch trout for dinner every day. I thought about how I would create a nature path down to the river. I owned two kayaks but never used them since it was a challenge to load them into a truck and transport them to a lake. Living here, I could just pick up a kayak and carry it to the pond across the street. I envisioned sitting on the front porch watching the cars go by or reading a good book by the river's edge. I felt as though every day that someone else lived in my house was exempting me from living my own dream. I wondered if I would ever get the chance to experience it.

Chapter 11

Meeting my Nemesis

With my daily exercise walks up and down Pinhook Road, I became curious about the neighboring graveyard. It was so old and inviting and had many very old stone tablets. Every once in a while I would take a stroll through the historic burial ground just to read the poetic epitaphs. There were young and old here. One particular set of headstones marked a family plot with their three children who all died very young. In the span of just five years, between 1845 and 1850, the Knight family was decimated. A daughter named Mary, aged fifteen years and eleven months, passed away only three days before Christmas. This is the heart-rending missive that is inscribed into the lower half of her old and weathered headstone.

"Short was thy years, Sweet the date,

Meeting thy savior at the gate.

How shortly thou dids't resign thy breath,

At the hands of cruel death."

After a few minutes of trying to come to grips with this poor family's loss, I moved on, perusing the stream edge of the graveyard, reading the names of other patriots and pioneers. All of a sudden, a name I read hit me like a splash of ice water to my face. There was the man who left no clear records for me to find in the archives, the man who once held the ownership to my lot, and the man whom I had just filed legal action against. There was the man who cost me over one-thousand dollars and the lost sale of my home.

Osbourne's grave site sat only seven rows back from my knoll. I wanted to scream, "What were you thinking," but out of respect for his wife Ruth and their young daughter buried beside them, I just walked away disquieted. I had lost the sale of the home because of a lack of clarity in the records. I had to spend money I didn't have to hire a lawyer, and now I was lost as to what would ultimately become of this place. I felt adrift in a sea of confusion as I wandered back to my house questioning everything I thought I understood about pursuing your dreams and never giving up. My dreams had collapsed under the piled up weight of discouragement.

The following week, after over two months of waiting, a letter arrived in the mail from my lawyer. I assumed it was a bill or another hurdle in our saga of the white house's troubles. "Here we go again," I groaned. I opened the letter with a lot of trepidation and decided I should sit down to read it. It's just easier to absorb those body blows while you're sitting down. I read the letter which started with the words,

"Walter Bannon v. Osborne Chaplin,"

I took in a deep breath before flipping the fold to expose the next line.

"I am pleased to report that judgement has been entered in your favor."

"Yay and Hallelluia," I shouted. It was clear and absolute proof that I was the new legal owner of the land. Wow! This was good news. It helped to calm my fraying nerves.   I was ready to cry if I had to face another setback. This time I wanted to cry with the excitement of winning this round. This time things were different. I could inhale deeply without the pain from my chest surgery and I could exhale fully, leaving the weight of all of the previous problems to fade away like a warm breath that vanishes into a cold thin air. I knew what I needed to do next. I had to walk over to the cemetery now and apologize to Mr. Chaplin. I was feeling remorseful for having chided him in his final resting place. Reading his gravestone again, it hit me that he died at only forty-nine years old. He was around the age that I was when I first discovered my heart problems. I too could have left this world without the time to get my house in order. Perhaps he never expected to leave this world so young, and perhaps he never got around to many other things like land deeds and title filings. History books talk of a fire at the home of one of the early settlers who had kept records for the local residents. Perhaps those early deeds were destroyed too?

I later discovered that Osborne was given those burial plots on the river side of the cemetery in exchange for building a fence at both ends of the cemetery in 1855 (Bridgton News). It seems that he actually did a lot of work on the graveyard to ensure a proper resting place for himself, his family, and many others in this place of peace. After his contribution to the beauty of the cemetery, he was given options to use a twenty foot extension on the side near the brook in whatever manner he desired. It is apparent now that he chose to be buried with his family on the river edge overlooking his early wood-mill below. I forgave him and his silent response was humbling. Mr. Chaplain and I made our peace. I walked away comforted and he continued his eternal rest without any more interruptions from me.

SANDY
CREEK
CEMETERY

Chapter 12

The Day the Stars Aligned

Our first tenant stayed for two years after which two graduate students rented for a year. Following them another tenant rented the home for six years, and over that course of time, I completed many upgrades to the little home. We always made sure the improvements to the house were changes that we would like to see if we were living there, not that there were any plans for us to ever move into the house. It was just easier to outfit and renovate it with the concept of what it would look like if we were tenants.

The little house carried its own weight with respect to the expenses verses the income. While I still would have preferred to be the one living in the cozy little home on the knoll, I had to at least feel good that it was making someone else a lovely residence and, on the positive side of things, it would eventually pay off its own mortgage and provide a positive income flow for us. With the small home-equity line of credit we had on it, it wouldn't take many years to close out the debt completely.

Everything began to change, however, when the tenant said that she needed to speak with us. I was used to getting calls about maintenance issues like "The smoke detector keeps beeping" or, "The faucet is leaking," but this sounded like a different issue altogether. Something was up and we would find out within the week.

A few days on, my wife met with her and was told that, sadly, she would be leaving the little white house in July. That would be in just a couple of months. This created urgency for us. If the house didn't have a tenant, we would be left to pay the insurance, taxes, heat, electricity, water, and the loan, without the income that normally took care of all of that. We decided to explore the option of renting it through an on-line short term program. It seemed like a great option. We owned enough household items to furnish most of the house, except that a couple of new mattresses and couches would need to be purchased. We could then rent it by the day or by the week. This appeared to be our best move. That would not only cover the expenses of the home, it would also leave certain weeks open for our own family to be able to stay while they were visiting us.

We agreed that this direction was the best option and began to set the home up for weekly rental use. Every improvement, including things as minute as the new coffee pot, relied on the concept that it would be the way we would like it if we lived here. We added a front sitting deck that looked out over the pond at the front of the knoll. We had already put a new deck in the back facing the stream and the cemetery, but we added a cute table and chair set there too. We began to add shrubs and flowers to line the walkways. Inside, we trimmed out the ceilings, added nice flooring to the bedrooms, and installed a second bathroom upstairs. The electrician returned to check all of the smoke detectors and activate new outlets in the upstairs bathroom. My kids even bought us a full set of white towels to accommodate the weekend renters. Finally, after months of preparing the knoll-house for vacationers, we were ready to roll!

I was enjoying this part of the growth of the home. It just felt like the final touches of a beautiful portrait were being applied to our canvas. It reminded me of the world-famous Michelangelo painting where God's finger touches man's finger. We were placing our final touch on the irresistible house that we would list on the internet within days. The new motif included prints of the old two-foot railroad cars that used to pass through Sandy Creek every day in the early years. We had lamps that were old railroad station styled, and cute little Maine-Aroostock model trains sitting on a perch above the staircase's overhang. I toyed with the idea of placing a large yellow and black "Rail-Road-Crossing" sign at the corner of the yard but I knew that the more measured half of my partnership would tell me to, "Keep it within the rails!" The house was so adorable now. I felt that vacationers would love it so much they'd never want to leave it. I envied them already.

It was at this point that an unexpected twist in our perfectly laid out plans occurred. My daughter needed to find a place to live for the summer for her family of five. Their home had sold much quicker than anticipated, and while they waited for their new home to be built, they would have to find a temporary residence. We were more than thrilled to have them come this way and use the little home we had just gotten all dolled up for a date. At first it seemed like a logical step to just have them live in the rental house, but the fact that there were five of them and only two of us, led us to discuss the possibility of them using our three-bedroom home while my wife and I would stay at the smaller rental house. Albeit, it would only be temporary, it would suit both of our families much better. Since we had just been setting up the home to match our liking, moving just down the street into it would be simple, and it would provide us a pleasant opportunity to experience what it felt like to live in the darling doll-house on the top of knoll.

Have you ever felt like all of the stars have been aligned just for you? Or maybe you've had a situation like planning a party for someone, then you get to the party and when you see the cake and all of the decorations, it hits you. The party you were working on was secretly your own! I had this underlying feeling that things could be heading this way, but it was not something my wife was willing to consider at this time. Not wanting to be presumptuous or contentious, I rarely brought up the possibility of us staying in the rental for a longer period. Whenever I tried to slip the idea into our conversations, it was usually met with snippets of skepticism.

"There would have to be so much done to make this house our home," she would often say. "I would need more closets, a dormer would need to be built, and I'd need a sewing room."

It was better to leave the subject alone because there was no way I wanted to get a loan for another upgrade to the house that would cost tens of thousands of dollars. I was ready to stop remodeling and to start living!

We made the move pretty quickly once it was agreed upon as to which family would live where. As time passed, we began to create small ways to fit our belongings from our other home into the rental house. Each nook and cranny became a place to hold something we wanted or needed here. The basement had never been completed. It still had bare cement walls and a bare floor so we discussed a plan to add three closets into that downstairs portion of the house. This would remove the need to raise the roof. It would add living space and save us a lot of money, since finishing the basement would only cost us about five-thousand dollars verses a twenty-thousand dollar dormer. I was becoming skilled to the point of confidence with a hammer and power tools so I figured that I could frame in the walls with a little help from my son-in-law. I could manage insulating the walls myself, then I could hire a sheetrock professional to complete the walls. I knew enough about flooring to install a floor and, in a couple of months it could add a third more living space to the house. This plan made my wife much more willing to consider staying here for a longer term. We both felt that, regardless of what the outcome was to be, this would be a good improvement to make. We also agreed that it should start right away.

The process of fitting into the little home was becoming a labor of love. We began to give away clothing and items we really didn't need. This actually felt very good. We discovered that minimalizing and downsizing are very rewarding tasks. We started to feel pleased with how comfortable we were becoming. One of the daily and quite comical challenges we faced was how we differentiated which house was which. We were calling one house "The Little House" and the other "The Big House." Then we called one house "Four-P," and the other "Thirty-Three-P." I started to toss around some easier terms to help everyone know one from the other. "Small House, Big House" just didn't fit the bill since one wasn't actually small, nor was the other one big. Some friends even started to help me out with suggestions like "Pinhook Pleasure," "Love Landing," "Castle Crest," "The Railroad House," and "Riverside Rest."

Many other unbearable names were tossed out for our consideration but nothing stuck. Then one day out of the blue my wife proposed we call it "Brookside." I liked it. It was simple. It had an easy charm to it and, best of all, it meant she was starting to warm up to her new digs.

Relieved at our agreement on a name my brother jumped at the opportunity to help put an end to our squabbles over a missing moniker. He soon delivered to us a wooden-lettered sign to hang on the front of our house.

"Brookside"

It was now set into the history of this home's transformation. The home on the hill finally had a name. This created another problem however. What do we call the other house? "Big House" wasn't good anymore since the name "Little House" was gone. In no time flat, I heard that same creative woman who came up with "Brookside" blurt out "Homestead." It made sense and was again simple and fitting. It was settled. We lived at Brookside and my kids lived at Homestead. Now all I needed was a carved plaque to hang on their house.

Due to unforeseen circumstances, Homestead was going to be occupied substantially longer than originally thought. That meant that we would be at

Brookside for a longer time too. In my mind it meant that we were here for good. I was feeling pretty sure this was going to be a final move. It was slowly becoming a possibility for my wife too. Every time we used a little nook to figure out how to accommodate another need, in my mind it simply strengthened the likelihood that we were here to stay.   My wife's level of approval was at about eighty percent and growing daily. She often stated, in a sort of accepting way, that there were a couple of things that we needed to address if we were to make this our actual home. I was always ready to listen and quick to act!

In the meantime, we brought our kayaks to Brookside. We started taking adventures up the pond all the way to the headwaters at old Hensborough where Mr. Snapper and Mrs. Heron were still enjoying the tranquil waters. I started clearing a footpath to the stream edge ending at a spot to cast my fishing lures. Every day we were discovering new aspects of what life was like living at Brookside. The morning sunshine to the golden sunsets proved a blessing beyond measure.

Another positive I discovered was that living at

Brookside was starting to turn me into an historian of sorts. I'd been reading article after article on the history of the Free Will Baptists that held church services on this very spot. I recognized many of the names in the membership records as being similar to the names in the neighboring cemetery. The Bridgton Historical Society gave me a copy of a picture from a 1909 news story of sisters whose father was the minister here in 1854. It showed what the church building looked like back in the mid-nineteenth century. It is shocking to realize that it would be hard to tell the difference from that first building to today's Brookside. It's almost as though the original building was put back up. How perfectly coincidental!

The article also included a list of the old hymns they sang and how the organ and pews were arranged. It mentioned two doors at the entry for the purpose of separating the men and women entering the church building. According to the article, the building was often filled to capacity as a church and later as a community center with dinners, musical events, and Creek meetings (Bridgton News Jan.24, 1909, p.1).

"In Bridgton Again After 50 Years" Bridgton News, 24 January 1909. p. 1.

Chapter 13

Who Knew

While moving into Brookside was unplanned, it actually has been a dream come true. I sure didn't see it coming. I looked at the purchase of the land as an opportunity to create something enjoyable. I never planned to set up my retirement home here. If I could have seen the whole picture of how events were going to unfold, I am certain we would have never undertaken this crazy project. I really don't believe that things like this just happen by chance though, and although I don't wish to sound too ethereal, I have to believe that there was a divine intervention in the entire process.

A good example of this is when I was sitting in the living room one afternoon, relaxing and soaking up a bit of the short sunlight that this house gets in the winter. After months of remodeling Brookside, I was trying to retreat a bit from all the busy work. My wife and I both needed to start adjusting to living in our new shell with all of its pros and cons. Sitting alone one afternoon, I started to muse over what would be good improvements to make for the future of this home. Staring out my window, one thought I had immediately was how wonderful it would be to get rid of the two huge pine trees that were blocking the sun for three to four hours of the best part of the day. I wished that they were on my land so that I could just chop them down; unfortunately, they sat on my neighbor's lot. With those trees gone, it would be like having an endless supply of propane in my tank. Any solar warming you can get is very advantageous during the cold winter months in Maine.

"Oh Lord, if I could only have that sun for just a

few more hours a day, I would be very happy here, you know," I bemoaned.

In any case, the fact that this little home had so much that I loved about it meant that I was still perfectly happy to accept living here with a few less-than-perfect remaining issues. Still unsettled about this problem, I grabbed my coat and exited the side door to look at the one tree in my own yard that worried me because it leaned towards the house. I hated that it dropped pine-cones on the roof all the time. It also delivered pine sap to all of our porch furniture in the summer. If it fell during a storm, it could easily come through the roof and into the bedroom. That made sleeping very tenuous on windy nights.

While I was walking around the outside of the house looking at the trees, I thought that I heard someone calling my name. "Walter," the voice whispered. I looked around and didn't see anyone and assumed it was all in my mind, or maybe it was the whistling wind. A minute later I heard it again a bit stronger this time. "Walter." It was definitely my name being called. I spun around a full 360 degrees wondering who was playing games with me. I looked up and down the street and then I looked up at the sky. It was then that I heard somebody chuckling at me. It was my neighbor calling over to me. Her head barely topped the shrubbery edging her driveway. She walked over to the brim of her yard, and I did the same in mine. Speaking from across the road she asked if I'd be willing to give her some professional advice.

Now I have to say, there are not many things that I would be able to offer professional advice on, but I offered to do my best.

She then asked if I thought that she should remove the two huge pine trees that shrouded the sun from a large area of her yard. I had to laugh at first, and then I advised her that I could give her two opinions. One would be based on reason, and the other based on a more selfish outcome. That selfish one was what I shared first!

She looked puzzled at that odd comeback, and then I explained to her how I had just been agonizing over those two trees. She chuckled again. After she heard me share how those giant old pines were blocking hours of precious winter sunlight from my home as well, and how much I would love to see them removed, she proclaimed immediately, "I have made my decision." She decided that she was going to have them taken down. I told her she needn't cut them down for my sake but that she should do what was best for her situation. She hadn't even heard my second opinion but at this point, it was moot. She resolved to act on my first point of advice.

We spent the next half-hour looking at how they were keeping her roof and back yard from getting that precious morning sun. She was now confident that the trees needed to go and I was pleased as pie to know they were going. We settled on having both of them removed within the week. The best part of it all was that this improvement wasn't going to cost me a penny! As for my tree, I figured on having the same tree-fellers that were going to remove hers remove mine as well.

I walked back to Brookside with a smile that just wouldn't stop. I was anxious to tell my wife the good news when she arrived home from work. I figured that this just might be the news that would bring her approval rating from eighty percent to one-hundred percent. It certainly did remove my short bout with ambivalence. With a reverent finger pointed to the sky, I simply whispered, "Thank you!"

Another interesting post-move twist was when I called a contractor to come and estimate the cost to take the sand from the driveway and replace it with crushed stone. Ten minutes after he'd arrived, we were discussing the costs and the options I had when, in the middle of a sentence, he stopped talking, looked at the home with his head cocked to one side and asked, "Where did this house come from, did you build it…I mean, did you….." he stuttered.

I began to tell him that I had moved it from North Windham and he again stopped me.

"I thought it looked familiar," he replied, shaking his head in disbelief. "I used to play in this house when it was in Windham because we were friends of the owners." He told me their names and continued, "I helped clean it out when the owners moved out years ago."

After learning that new information about this

home I felt that it would be standard protocol to give him a tour of the inside, as I've done for all the others who've been curious. He was very eager to see it. Walking room to room, he was delighted and astonished at the house's transformation. He seemed thrilled to be taking part in welcoming this home to Sandy Creek. I enjoyed watching his wide-eyed expressions as he recalled what it used to look like in his youth.

"This was the bathroom," he chortled as he discovered that we had made that tiny space into a laundry room. Perhaps he recalled how funny it was to be able to use the commode and wash your hands at the same time? Each time we entered another area of the house he had a recollection that made him smile from ear to ear. He could hardly believe he was seeing the same home of his childhood playground now re-established in his own neighborhood. That showing remains one of the favorite tours I have given since the home landed here on that crazy morning. It was yet another one of the many ironic encounters that I have been happy to share with yet one more intrigued visitor.

Each warm sunrise and brilliant sunset now

attests to the fact that this was surely a great course of events planned out, I believe, even before I had handed in my excessive bid. Each morning I push the curtains as far apart as is possible to give the sun plenty of space to do its job. The couch warms up like an electric blanket and the floors take in the sunshine and generate warmth for our feet. Then in the evening I check the red-shaded sky from the southern horizon all the way across to its western setting. The pink colors touch the steeple on the church and the homes high enough to be splashed with the gentle hue of the day's end.

The transformation of this home from day one to now is an uncanny, yet wonderful evolution. This barren fortress of long ago, destined for destruction, has come back to life to provide warmth and comfort to our family and others for perhaps another one hundred years. It's a very strong structure. It's dry, warm, and super cozy. With a few other minor tweaks, we'll have the retirement home we could only have dreamed of. Who knew?

Chapter 14

Shambles to Shamballa

This white house now speaks without words from her new perch. Like a proud loon's call reverberates across a peaceful Maine lake on a warm summer day, this knoll-top house echoes the voices of two-hundred and fifty years of mothers and fathers who wielded mere axes and saws to clear spaces for their expeditious young families. They bared this little hilltop at the epicenter of this front-runner community they first called Pinhook, and later re-named Sandy Creek. They built a meeting house here and used it to assemble those hearty folks for gatherings of all types. Most of those early settlers lie in silence just a few yards from Brookside's back yard. They are like guards at the gate protecting the memories of the past, reminding all who visit how challenging life was at this community's beginnings. Their epitaphs are their history books. Their enduring stories exist only in what we still see today all around us. It's in the buildings, the wildly strewn stones littering the river bed below, the granite dam, and the many stone walls cresting every rise.

I feel as though I've inserted myself into the common history of this village by placing a dwelling on this perch. Consequently, I feel a responsibility to carry the torch forward. "Don't let the flame die," seems to echo from the woodlands surrounding this knoll. I trust that in this whole process of walking blindly into our setting-sun abode and adding our fingerprints onto the mural of time that some good has been created here for others to embrace. Like Osborne, who made the graveyard a fine place of rest for many, my hopes are that Brookside will be a place of warmth and comfort for years to come for many too.

May this once busy hilltop that hosted a house of inspiration for so many of Sandy Creek's early citizens be an enduring beacon to all who pass her by today. I'll turn the porch light on to remind those travelers of the importance of this knoll and I'll leave it on to the memory of those bygone settlers who sacrificed the comforts of Massachusetts to resettle here and begin life anew. I'll visit their memorials often and thank them for being courageous enough to make this dream of theirs a reality, which in turn, has helped make my dream come true.

"Would I do this again?" I get asked. I can't honestly answer yes or no because this journey has been both wonderful and difficult for both of us. I know for certain what my spouse's response would be though.

In my daily drives now, I still notice little land parcels for sale here and there, and I often consider making an offer on them just in case I see another free house somewhere crying out for a second chance to become a loving home. So while every ramshackle building I pass day in and day out screams out, "Take

Me," I have to fight the voices in my mind and force my eyes to look the other away. In poker they say that you've got to know when to hold them and when to fold them. While I still love the idea of turning something from shambles into my Shamballa, I also need to be thankful that I survived this venture. I can feel secure in closing the book on this chapter in my life.

I have been blessed to have experienced many historic pearls with our move to this hilltop. I truly love every aspect of this old home's charm as well. I know a house is only made of wood, plastic and many other materials held together by a million nails, yet each nail was placed by carpenters' skilled hands. The sweat, the tears, and even sometimes the blood of the worker is stained forever into the fabric of that shelter. Some would say that a home is actually a whole lot more than just artfully assembled building supplies. Can wood, paint, mortar, bricks, and glass, think or feel? Of course not! Nonetheless, they'll suggest that when all of these elements are assembled together to hold back the oft cruelness of Mother Nature, then a house becomes more than a building. It becomes a home.

I do believe that a home is more than brick and mortar, and once it is lived in it becomes a breathing extension of the many lives that have entered it. A home captures the heart of the dreamers who built it and shares that dream with everyone invited to enter its portals. Their voices echo forever through the wood frames and stone walkways. Their songs never completely fade away.

I embrace my new surroundings with an entirely new appreciation now. The only thing I have not yet embraced with this home is the way it rumbles like an earthquake when a heavy build-up of ice and snow comes sliding off of the metal roof and crashes onto the patio below. It starts off sounding like a Narrow-Gauge train running through my house, and then it ends with a torrent of thuds. I suppose however that this too will someday become music to my ears. Until then, I'll sit comfortably ensconced in my new surroundings with an appreciation for history and for those in whose paths I now walk. Living in the Little White House is a dream-come-true that, like many things in life, had to be let go, to return, and then become reality. Yes, the challenges were myriad, but the contentment of living here validates in me that it was worth all of the trials along the way.

ABOUT THE AUTHOR

Walter W. Bannon has written two books prior to writing *Tales of a Little White House*. *The White Pocketbook* allowed readers a look into his mother's amazing survival of WWII as a young Belgian girl while his book, *Digger Down,* shares the zany experiences during his antique bottle hunting adventures in Maine. He and his wife reside in Cumberland County where he enjoys writing and performing Irish music, as well as giving lectures on his books.

Works Cited

Bridgton Historical Society. Bridgton, Maine 1768-1994 An updated Bicentennial History. 1993.   p.24,p.340,p.496.

 "In Bridgton again after 50 years." Bridgton News, 24 January 1909. p. 1.

"Fencing The Burial Ground Seemed To Be One Of Troublesome Problems." Bridgton News-second installment 1909.

www.ingramcontent.com/pod-product-compliance
Lightning Source LLC
Chambersburg PA
CBHW071521150726
48000CB00002B/630